T0064118

Extraordinary Women – Singapore

Extraordinary Women – Singapore

Karen Lee

PARTRIDGE
A Penguin Random House Company

To order additional copies of this book, contact
Toll Free 800 101 2657 (Singapore)
Toll Free 1 800 81 7340 (Malaysia)
orders.singapore@partridgepublishing.com

www.partridgepublishing.com/singapore

CONTENTS

FOREWORD

Gender stereotypes.

What is so typical of a gender that makes people form firm illusions or prejudice, one against another? Do not get me wrong, I have nothing but admiration for any gender who makes their own honest living and in so doing, keeps their own dignity and earns their own respect. The situation that is baffling me is the traditional prejudice which former generations have instilled in women and that gender inequality starkly exists in many first-world societies even till today. Moving forward, there are also stifling questions as to how women can achieve equal standing with their male counterpart.

I came across an article in *Vogue* magazine entitled **"Breaking The Silicon Ceiling"**, which, as the title suggests is about women engineers in the Silicon Valley. The story is narrated by Tracy Chou, a computer scientist working with Pinterest. Prior to that, she was on internships at Facebook and Google before taking on a foundational role at Quora.

For many years, Tracy had been intensely aware of the complaints about technology firms employing fewer and fewer female engineers. She had no concrete proof of the figures even though it was in plain sight and decided to deal head-on with the nagging problem in technology firms, which was the severe shortage of women in the ranks of engineering roles. At the annual gathering of female technologists called the Grace Hopper Celebration, Tracy brought to the problem of missing data of women in engineering roles and she wrote a blog post on *medium.com* to call for all technology companies to submit the number of female engineers employed by their companies respectively in the Silicon Valley.

The numbers that came into Tracy's database were atrocious and unacceptable. At Facebook, women made up only 17 percent of their tech team. At Facebook and Yahoo, the numbers of women in their tech team were at an even lower at 15 percent. The atrocious numbers in the tech industry are much worse off than the numbers in the finance and entertainment sectors.

Sociologists try to make sense of the low numbers and they asked distinctive and pertinent questions like, "Are women less intelligent than men?" No. "Are they less responsible in their jobs?" No. "Do women have less aptitude than their counterparts?" No. "Do women have less empathy, less ability, to comprehend their work tasks at hand, to answer to customer queries, to be less competent employees as men?" No. Vivek Wadwa, an entrepreneur researcher and now a fellow with Stanford University, interviewed hundreds of women in the technology sector in preparation for his new book "**Innovating Women: The Changing Face of Technology**". The dismal number of female programmers and engineers in top technology firms caught him by surprise and he was shocked with the pathetic number of women employed by technology firms and the C-level Executives who are not even concerned with such disparity.

Sheryl Sanberg's book "**Lean In**" was a bold and stark reminder to all women that they should lean in, step up and take leadership roles. She reiterates that it is not alright to be discounted by men at work and at Board meetings. Women should cultivate self-confidence and not back down when a difficult project is given to them. For decades, men were considered the provider, decisive and driver. On the other hand, women are characterized as being the caregivers, sensitive and communal. Therefore, if a woman climbs the career ladder, focusing on building her career and gaining power at their workplace, they are frown upon. This is the old-fashioned stereotypical expectations of women.

In recent times, many celebrities have also stepped up to call for equality between two genders and one of them is Emma Watson, who shot to fame with her character Hermione Granger in the Harry Potter films. Watson is also a goodwill ambassador for the UN and she urges more men and boys to take a stand and support women's rights. Emma Watson also used the International Women's Day to act as a catalyst for the HeForShe campaign which was launched in September last year and inspires men and boys to join the cause to fight for equal rights. To date, there are about 240,000 men have pledged their commitment online in accordance to the HeForShe website and they include U.S. President Barack Obama and actor Matt Damon. The HeForShe website also targets to mobilise one billion men and boys by July this year.

On our sunny island, women particularly those who are in the workforce, are faced with balancing their traditional and modern-day roles in Singaporean society and economy. Firstly, Singapore's society expects women to become creative and prolific corporate workers and they are also expected to play the role of traditional women in the household, especially as a wife and mother. Secondly, Singaporean women are conflicted between work and family, which poses as the greatest challenge for women in Singapore's workforce. Singapore's female managers are reportedly fewer in number despite the fact that many women managers have gone through college education and are no longer illiterate. Many have even completed their post-graduate studies but have decided to stay at home after giving birth to their children, hoping to nurture and inculcate the "right" or "expected" moral values to their children.

For years, Singapore has been trying to justify and resolve the gender inequality. In 1961, the Women's Charter Act was passed so as to improve and protect the rights of women in Singapore and to guarantee greater legal equality for women in legally sanctioned relationships. The Act administers and caters to the institution of monogamous marriages, the rights of husbands and wives in marriage, to safeguard and provide for family stability, and to answer to the potential legal complexity with regard to divorce and separation settlement.

The Women's Charter helps protect women from sanctioned marriages in Singapore. However, it does not address the intrinsic issue of gender inequality in our first-world nation which functions more like an age-old Confucius society. Gender inequality is prevalent in across all job functions. Women faced indiscrimination in aspects of salary, promotion, leadership and also explicit sexual harassment in the workplace, which most hope to cover up than to blow the whistle because these women are afraid of discrimination and the worst thing will be to lose their jobs.

AWARE, or Association of Women for Action and Research, is a non-governmental organization in Singapore which was established in November 1985 to promote gender equality. This non-governmental group has taken action, spoken aloud and brought our attention about gender inequality. However, the membership in AWARE is a mere 550 persons since its inception. AWARE has been involved in assisting rape victims, women violated and beaten by their husbands and anti-human trafficking. The organisation has even dwell on the subject of helping women who are contemplating of abortion. For years, AWARE has been trying to make a difference and it has looked at policies to help alleviate the wretched status of women in Singapore.

According to Singapore's Ministry of Manpower (MOM), women make up over 45% of Singapore's workforce. Despite of this huge percentage, many women continue to face various factors that curb and obstruct their full career advancement. AWARE has voiced out that it is necessary that the MOM and AWARE work together to address the dire situation of women's status in the workforce and articulate the requirement to accelerate and advance gender equality in the workplace.

It is often said that if we, as women, want to be treated more fairly in the society, we will need to acknowledge the fact that we can do it as well as men or even better. Self-confidence plays a huge role in this aspect. Like MOM and AWARE, we need government bodies and institutions to notice and rectify this traditional behaviour by championing more women, calling them to take action, to ask questions, to speak louder, to take on challenging roles and to fight for their own rights. When the women population recognizes that we have the capability to trudge forward and that we are adequate, or even more proficient, at managing and handling the same kind of roles and stress levels, only then we can accelerate the progress of gender equality.

It is not my desire or intent to further delve on the issue of gender inequality as these would be repeatedly discussed amongst the various forums, institutions and organizations who are advocates in this area. Rather, it dawned onto me that there are women who have excelled in their own areas of expertise, gone through tough life struggles and ultimate successes, and it would be great to know these women, how they have done it and what examples, right or wrongly, can we learn from them.

My book is a compilation of interviews with Singaporean women who have balanced their work and family life extremely well. They provide excellent examples for women who are struggling to balance both their jobs and family. It took me two years to complete the interviews and I would sincerely like to thank the interviewees for taking time off their already busy schedule in answering my questions.

Hopefully, the content will inspire and motivate women in Singapore who wishes to earn her own living, with dignity and respect, as a woman, wife or mother. Keep an open mind and keep an open heart.

Ms Claire Chiang

Super Mom, Super Wife and Super Entrepreneur

I met Mr. Ho Kwon Ping in 2000 when he was a speaker at a White Collar Crime Fighting Conference. Although he was a well-known business leader, I saw a very humble and down-to-earth businessman. We had designated escorts from the Singapore Police Force to guide the speakers around the exhibition hall but Mr. Ho declined having one and preferred to walk around the exhibition hall himself. Although he had achieved a lot in life, his quiet persona and down-to-earth personality made me wonder about the woman behind this successful businessman.

Ms Claire Chiang, the spouse of Mr. Ho Kwon Ping, comes across to me as a stoic "Iron Lady". I have never met her before but I have read many articles which personified "Iron Lady" Ms Chiang to be a gutsy, motivated and very determined businesswoman. Most of the articles talk about Ms Chiang's achievements in the business arena, her conviction to feminism and her determination and strong desire to make life and business work. I did not want to read about Ms Chiang from the articles. I wanted to hear this "Iron Lady" speak and share her own life and business experiences.

So when I found out that Ms Chiang was going to be one of the speakers at "Can Women Have It All?" forum organized by Mums@work, I jumped at the chance to listen to this female business leader speak and of course, to meet her in real life. True to words and articles written about Ms Chiang, she was every bit the devoted business leader who had a very strong conviction for life.

When she spoke, I listened intensely because her speech was thought–provoking. She did not speak about her achievements but shared on how to balance life, work and motherhood. She was providing us, the younger women entrepreneurs at the forum insights on "how to have it all" by drawing from her own experiences. I told myself I must get an interview with Ms Chiang and wrote in to Banyan Tree Holdings directly. To my elation, Ms Chiang readily agreed to do the interview.

Much of what she says in my interview with her comes from her own life experiences, her sacrifices and her triumph to get people to sit up and listen to what she needs to say. You can say she is a true motivational speaker. She is also one of the pioneer women entrepreneurs and one of the two women in 89 years of history to be admitted to the Singapore Chinese Chamber of Commerce and Industry. As an NMP, Ms Chiang also raised many issues in Parliament related to the social service sector, women, family, education and the disadvantaged.

The interview which I did with Ms Chiang features a softer side of her as a mother and wife and how she runs her household. I asked her many personal questions from her pregnancy to being a mother, a wife, and then a business leader and how she managed to juggle so many hats at one time. She was very candid and kind to answer the questions forthrightly, making the interview really interesting and captivating at the same time. Super mom, super wife and super entrepreneur — Ms Claire Chiang.

The interview

Q1.   Why did you choose sociology as a major in University? Did you actually want to do something else?

I was accepted to the law faculty but decided against it as I was told it was a cut and dry discipline and did not fit with my personality. Sociology has provided me with a broader and more insightful perspective on how business, society and government work.

Q2.   You have a very strong conviction to feminism and a great passion for life. Was this shaped by your early formative years? Did your parents inculcate this conviction and passion in you?

It is a journey of awareness, sharpened by travel, reading, and engagement in community efforts. As a working woman, wife and mother, now social activist, you cannot but become clearer about the important role women play in shaping and defining gender relations and defining the notion of what constitutes a good society. We have our views, and they should be heard and included in all political discourse. Although my parents are traditional, they gave me the room to express and find myself by supporting all my engagements.

Q3. Although your family was not rich, your mother made sure that you had a proper and good education to give you a good start in life, what do you think about this?

I think that is the best thing a mother can do for her daughter. Despite limited opportunity on her own behalf, my mother ensured I completed my tertiary education which to her was a symbol of the lifeline for my personal development.

Q4. You became a human resource director in your husband's company, why did you leave to set up your own business?

I was co-founder of Banyan Tree and in my job I continue to guide the human capital planning and development while taking on other roles.

Q5. Why were you enthralled by the spa business? Was it something you have always wanted to do, to house travelers, give them a wonderful and relaxing time and also help local businesses?

I think of spa as a "Self Pampering Art." As part of the Banyan Tree wellness experience, our spas are a vital part of the guest experience as many come to our resorts to rejuvenate and enjoy a moment of stillness from their hectic daily lives. The spas are an extension of the concept of Banyan Tree, which shelters travelers and provides a space for respite.

Q6. Your company is now a multi-million dollar organization because of your conviction and business acumen, how do you feel about achieving so much?

This is not just a product of my own effort. My husband, Ho Kwon Ping, is the visionary leader, supported by a wonderful team of architects and our property-based staff which now numbers 9,500 associates from 59 countries. We have expanded into different brands, including Banyan Tree's sister brand, Angsana, and it is really the collective journey of achievement for which we are most grateful.

Q7. What was your first reaction when you knew you were going to be a mommy?

Exhilaration! Motherhood is a unique experience that only a mother to be goes through.

Q8. Were you prepared for your pregnancy?

Yes, I was already 30 when I planned for my pregnancy, which at our time was considered rather late. I did all the necessary medical tests, and read thoroughly to prepare myself mentally for the baby.

Q9. Was your husband supportive during the pregnancy?

He was very involved and supportive. We were on our own in a small 2-room apartment without any help. This was very much a shared experience which I feel is a very important journey for a new mother to be.

Q10. Were you prepared for your own childbirth?

No, I went to birth classes in Thomson Medical Centre, without reading about or anticipating a Caesarean birth. After many hours of labor, the doctor decided that C-section was necessary for my own safety and that of my child. Kwon Ping rushed to a bookshop to read up on the topic straightaway.

Q11. How have things changed for you after you have become a mother?

Motherhood is the critical milestone for any woman because you become responsible for a vulnerable young person whom you have to also raise. Motherhood teaches you all the qualities required for protecting and nurturing others. It also gives you a perspective about family and draws you out from your own self-centredness.

Q12. Did you stop working after your first child was born so that you could be with him during his formative years?

Yes, I consciously took two years off from work because I did not have a helper, and I took care of my first child as I wanted to learn all about motherhood from breastfeeding to making baby food through motivating infants. Those years prepared me to be a competent mother while I continued to read, write and travel with my son. Motherhood did not stop me from being active; it became known that when friends invited me they also invited my son.

Q13. As a mother, what do you expect from your children? Are you a Tiger Mom?

The definition of a Tiger Mother is relative. Many would think I am a Tiger Mother because I do exercise discipline. The only expectation I have from my children is that they try and do their best. If they have tried, and failed, I have no issue. If they do not even try, and give excuses, that's when the Tiger rears its head and snarls.

Q14. What type of education did your children have? What do you think of the local school education system? Do you think our Singaporean children are having a well-rounded education?

All three children went to Nan Hua Primary School because I wanted them to have a Chinese education. My eldest went on to Hwa Chong Institution and then Hwa Chong Junior College; later to The Wharton School at the University in Pennsylvania to complete his education. My daughter went onto Raffles Girls' Secondary School followed by completing her degree at the London School of Economics. Ren Chun was enrolled at Anglo-Chinese School ("ACS") in an IB Programme and had since graduated. He is currently serving National Service. All three have different strengths and I do think the local school system could do less with examinations and grading, and do more with grounding our children in humanities and engaging them intensively in processes of discovery and experimentation in the world of the humanities. Let specialization come later. That said, parents are still the teachers in terms of life values and moral standards.

Q15.   How do you bond with your children? Do you have special moments or activities which you share with them?

Being the "Tiger Mom," I set up times for "meals of the day," "meals with grandparents," and "holiday planning." These are the non-negotiated family activities that they must be involved in though they are already 33 (Ren Hua), 30 (Ren Yung), and 21 (Ren Chun). Planning family activities and special moments require planning, determination and commitment. Parents must try to set up time, no matter how busy they are, for this process. They should invite the children to propose ideas. As long as children are interested in what you plan for them, they will enjoy being with you.

Q16.   Have you given up any great overseas job opportunities so that you can be a mother to 3 wonderful children and a wife to Mr Ho Kwon Ping?

Yes, I had to leave an engaging job in the faculty of medicine at HK University in order to return to Singapore with my husband after he was summoned following his father's stroke. We had just moved into and renovated an apartment in Hong Kong city after spending three years on Lama Island. Though unhappy about this need to move, my role as a wife at this juncture was a priority consideration. As it turned out, it was a turning point in my life journey.

Q17. You have an extremely tough and hectic work schedule as the Senior Vice-President of Banyan Tree Holdings, being a social activist, a volunteer, an entrepreneur and being appointed to sit on many Government and Education Boards, how do you ever find the time to spend with your children and your family?

Planning and commitment are two important exercises for a busy person. In 24 hours, and I need to only sleep for six, I have many hours to spread around in achieving "self bits," "marriage delights," "children's joy" and "work chunks." We can have it all!

Q18. You have made many firsts by breaking the norm for Singapore Women. You were one of first women to be elected to the Singapore Chinese Chamber of Commerce, how did you feel about the election? For many people, it is deemed a great achievement but is it difficult sitting in a Board Room with all male traditional Chinese business leaders? How do you make these men listen to what you want to say?

Many men in SCCC have said they would like their daughter to be like me but not their wife. You can imagine the anguish they would feel towards an independent woman like me. It's a matter of creating more opportunities and platforms for men and women to work together and feel comfortable with each other. I am grateful for that experience, to have helped to bridge that traditional ceiling, and made wonderful friendships in the Chinese Chamber, especially in leading the Career Women's Group for 16 years while being in charge of other committees. People, not just men, listen to what you want to say if you say it with reason, sincerity and integrity.

Q19. What advice do you have for Singaporean Women aspiring to be entrepreneurs and social activists like yourself?

A journey is 1000 steps, as the wise saying goes. You don't get to a destination by dreaming about it; you take the first step towards the direction now. You give time to achieving the goal.

II

Ms Claressa Monteiro

Music Extraordinaire

I thank Mark Zuckerberg. If you do not know him by now, he is the founder of *Facebook*. I was able to get connected with my friends and their friends and by a stroke of luck, one of them happens to be Singapore's renowned singer-songwriter, musician, host and super DJ, Ms Claressa Monteiro.

I set up Robe de Princesse, my new online web store and I was hugely surprised when Ms Monteiro had clicked "Like" on Robe de Princesse's Facebook page. I was even more astonished when she happily agreed to don my evening and cocktail dresses for her hosting events when I asked her. From the first time that Ms Monteiro adorned my black chiffon toga evening dress for her hosting gig, I knew she was a very friendly, honest and down-to-earth person. She is a shining star and I am just a new entrepreneur. I felt honoured and privileged to be given an opportunity to dress her.

It was hence a given that I had to invite Ms Monteiro to participate in *Extraordinary Women*. She was the prime example of one, juggling at least 6 facets of different roles, being a singer, songwriter, host, DJ, mother and wife, and standing tall in achieving all that she has. Ms Monteiro accepted the interview graciously and I was elated.

Ms Monteiro shared that she started vocal training as a child and her parents, who were fans of Nat King Cole, Louis Armstrong and Ella Fitzgerald, had exposed her to jazz music at a tender age. To her, jazz music was the sweetest and happiest music she had heard during her childhood. However, as a jazz singer, she now tends to stay away from the "tortured" jazz repertoire because to her, jazz music meant joy and sweetness.

I asked Ms Monteiro if she was a "born singer" or "trained singer". She was of the view that no matter how talented you are, to be successful as a musician, you need proper training. She opined that music education and application must take over, or else there might be no growth and development no matter how good your vocals are.

First and foremost a singer, Ms Monteiro wanted to explore being a DJ. She was given the golden opportunity when her A&R Manager at Universal Studio asked Bernard Lim if there was a space on his roster for her and the rest is history. Being a DJ, you are never far from music and in fact, you are also surrounded by music. As a DJ, you need to appreciate music, keep your cool under pressure and sound cheery and chirpy to all your listening fans whilst all hell might have broken loose in the recording studio.

In the interview, I asked Ms Monteiro many questions about motherhood and the first question was how she felt when she knew she was going to be a mom. Her answer was simple and it was "tears of joy". I also asked her if she was prepared for her pregnancy and she asserted that all pregnancies were unique and different for each mother-to-be, so no matter how many pregnancy guide books you might have read, you are never really ready to become a mother.

Ms Monteiro was very lucky and fortunate because her husband was extremely supportive to her during her pregnancies. He had even gone to the extent to beg for an Orange Julius at 1am in the early morning when Ms Monteiro had her cravings during pregnancy. Despite of all the care taken, she did not have easy labours and had to endure traumatic birth experiences for both her children. Nonetheless, all turned out good and she is very grateful to be able to have 2 wonderful children.

With children in her life, she revealed that she has become less self-centred and more willing to sacrifice, especially when it comes to her children. She gave up huge earning opportunities because she did not want to miss her children's first words, first steps and first day at school. After her second child was born, she even gave up her lucrative music career so that she could spend more time with her children. Everyone told her that being a housewife would kill her career, but she was of the view that she was a mother to her children first and career comes next. She stayed home for 4 years and returned to the music scene afterwards. It was difficult at first but with her sheer grit and hard work, and for many who believed in her like Ebel Watch, The Peak Magazine, The Ritz Carlton and also Universal Studio, she has become even more successful than before.

With her arduous and hard schedules, it seems Ms Monteiro needed 32 hours every day but she makes it work with 24. From the interview, I get strong vibes that Ms Monteiro is extremely proud of her two boys. As parents, she and her husband always taught their children to speak their minds, to be righteous and honest and that failure was not the end of the world and it was just a life lesson. She believes that her children, who are equipped with the values like honesty, truth, determination and without the fear of failing, will ultimately succeed and lead fulfilling lives. For Ms Monteiro, she expects nothing from her two children and her only hope for them is that they have no qualms about chasing their dreams, living their lives to the fullest and be happy.

Ms Monteiro wanted her children to be as Singaporean as they can be, so she enrolled them into local schools. She expects them to complete their National Service prior to talks of any overseas education. Ms Monteiro bonds with her children by spending her little free time with them in mind. She joins her children on the activities that they like to do, such as riding the most exhilarating rides at Universal Studio, cycling with them and getting all dirty by crawling all over the place in The Forest Adventure.

In 2002, she became the first South-East Asian music artiste to release her first jazz album entitled "Now and Then" with Universal Music. It would be a lifetime achievement for any local music artiste, but for Ms Monteiro, she felt very humbled and grateful by the opportunity given to her to release the album. She also stressed that whatever breaks she had, she had worked hard to achieve and deserve them and will continue doing so.

Ms Monteiro also related that she had given up many lucrative singing and contractual opportunities but the decision to give up came very naturally because for her, her boys and family always come first. Now that her children are much bigger, she feels a lot more balanced and at ease to chase after work opportunities before the sun sets down on her career.

In what most believe should be the pursuit of happiness, Ms Monteiro's happiness comes with the right pursuit.

III

Dr. Irene Chua

Caring & Dedicated Healthcare Provider

I was extremely fortunate to be granted an interview by a very popular Obstetrics and Gynaecology (O&G) Consultant, Dr Irene Chua, who runs her own medical practice at Gleneagles Medical Centre.

I first met Dr Chua when she was a still an O&G Senior Consultant at KK Children's & Women's Hospital (KKH). The first impression she gave me was that she was kind and easy to talk to, but under that gentle persona was a feisty, no-nonsense doctor and a straight-talker. Dr Chua is very passionate about her specialty and further to her blazing passion; she is a hard worker who is very knowledgeable about her field of studies. Before Dr Chua decided to leave KKH to open her own clinic at Gleneagles, she headed the 24-hour Obstetrics & Gynaecology clinic at KKH.

I was quietly impressed by this petite and pretty O&G doctor when she decided to set up her own O&G clinic at Gleneagles all by herself. If I was not that advanced in my pregnancy with my second son when I knew Dr Chua was going solo, she would definitely have been my O&G doctor, and if she were my O&G doctor, I wouldn't have put on 17kgs from my pregnancy.

This is because Dr Chua advocates that her patients watch their diet and have a good, sensible and safe exercise regime whilst pregnant. This helps to prevent her patients from succumbing to pre-natal blues and also to keep a healthy weight. With a healthy weight, her pregnant patients will be less predisposed to high-blood pressure and diabetes which can cause high risks in pregnancies.

When I first knew Dr Chua about 3 years ago, she was already a mother to Sophia. I have always been very fascinated and impressed by how female doctors handle their harsh work schedules with the mothering of their children and especially in O&G, when you are practically on call 24-hours because you really do not know when your patient is going to deliver. Even though it is such a tough specialty, Dr Chua feels that her vocation is a very happy one because they bring life into the world and O&G doctors help women sort out their infertility and gynaecology issues. The satisfaction comes from bringing life to Earth and also putting smiles on women's faces when their female factored issues have been resolved.

As an O&G doctor, I asked Dr Chua if she was happy when she found out that she was pregnant with Sophia and she said that,

"I was delighted at the prospect of being a mommy as we have been waiting 10 years for this day." And because Dr Chua was an O&G doctor and her pregnancy was very well-planned, she had a very smooth pregnancy without any hiccups. She even operated till the day she popped. But in reality, no one could ever be ready for one's child birth. Dr Chua started off with spontaneous labour only to end up in an emergency Caesarean section due to fetal bradycardia.

With Sophia in tow, Dr Chua reiterated that she has less time for herself these days as she spends most of her time with Sophia. With a hard schedule at work, she spends the little time she has away from work with her only daughter. When asked about the expectations she has on Sophia, Dr Chua related that she only wants Sophia to be happy and to have the best that she can provide.

When asked about Sophia's preschool education, Dr Chua disclosed that besides putting Sophia in Kindergarten, she has also enrolled Sophia into Chinese classes, drama classes, music classes and put Sophia into gym during the weekends. From Dr Chua's disclosure during interview, I can see that Sophia has a very well-rounded education and curriculum.

Dr Chua bonds with Sophia by engaging Sophia into everything that she does including bringing Sophia to work and when she makes her rounds at the hospital. I believe that by engaging Sophia with her work, Dr Chua hopes that her daughter will understand her mother much better.

I asked Dr Chua the reason behind setting up her own clinic and she replied that, "Sophia is one of the driving forces. The other is that I wanted to try something new, and to have something I can call my own." I guess all Momprenuers are the same. Their children are their inspiration and they want to run a business or venture that they can proudly call their own, even though it is tough being a Mompreneur when you have to call the shots both at work and at home.

Dr Chua expresses that she is much happier these days working for herself and having more time on her hands, which means she has more time to spend with her family and also with Sophia. Becoming a mother changes a woman's priority in life. When you have a child, you long to keep him or her company the whole day. This is because when you become a mother, your child is your whole world and you want to arrange your world and schedule around them.

Being a mother and an O&G Senior Consultant, I believe that Dr Chua understands her patients' needs more than anyone else and I am envious that her patients are in such good hands. I postulate that Dr Chua with her fearless personality and her hardworking and determined nature, her practice will undoubtedly flourish. On top of it, she can now give Sophia and her patients the required attention and the excellent healthcare service since she now runs her own business and is able to arrange and manage her own time schedule.

IV

The Art of Aesthetic Medicine

Dr Karen Soh is a doctor, a philanthropist, a businesswoman and a mother of 4 children. With so many responsibilities and a schedule more packed than a peak hour MRT train, you would appreciate that one would look more worn and tired than Gollum!

Instead, Dr Karen Soh, business owner and Medical Director of Privé Clinic, greeted me with a warm welcome and enamor during our interview that I felt extremely apologetic for taking so much of her already little free time. She was forthright and accommodating throughout the interview and shared her insights into her career, business and most importantly, family.

Dr Soh graduated from Raffles Girls' School and won the coveted Raffles Top Scholar Award. Since young, she already had a penchant to practice medicine. When asked if she was afraid of the gory of dissecting animals and humans for medical purposes, she smiled and said affirmatively, "No".

Dr Soh was trained in anaesthesia and intensive care for 5 years before she decided to become an aesthetic doctor. The 5 years of training in anaesthesia and intensive care taught Dr Soh to be a quick and intuitive thinker which assisted her in diagnosing and treating her patients with accurate clinical judgement. With Singapore's current exemplary and first-rate lifestyle, Dr Soh is quick to add that aesthetic medicine helps men and women look better and her patients always feel more confident after treatment.

Prior to opening her own practice, Dr Soh spent a year in Philadelphia, USA, where she developed a keen interest in anti-aging medicine. She also received her Board Certificate from The American Academy of Anti-Aging Medicine. Dr Soh set up her first clinic at Raffles Place and shifted to a bigger outfit at Palais Renaissance. I asked her if her clientele base has changed since the move and she responded that with the new clinic, the demographics of the clientele base have expanded to teenagers and ladies in their 90s!

Dr Soh feels that the winning strategy for any business, including hers, is about fair pricing pitched to market value. As her treatments and packages are affordable and managed by a very skilled doctor, her business saw an increase in clientele and amassed a huge following who became her loyal group of clients. This was also, no doubt, attributable to the quality of the treatment that the clinic brings to their clients.

According to Dr Soh, beauty is a composite of inner beauty, physical beauty and volumization. It also depends on the culture of the patient. For example, Caucasians will prefer a strong jawline whilst Asians hope to have an almond-shaped face.

Besides running her successful clinic, Dr Soh is also a mother of 4 children. She got married at 29 years old and got pregnant during her honeymoon. Dr Soh confessed that both she and her husband did not enjoy much of their "couple time" which many newlyweds did during the first few years of marriage. Dr Soh conceded that she was unprepared for her first pregnancy and childbirth and had to juggle with motherhood shortly after her marriage. Then again, how does one get prepared for parenthood?

Despite all the challenges that were posed and set forth to Dr Soh, she took everything in her stride. Her children are now aged 13, 10, 9 and 18 months and she adores them. She revealed that she has a team of competent staff who helps to relieve her workload. Since the business has stabilized, Dr Soh manages to spend more quality time with her family. Family time can be as simple as watching a movie together, going on vacation during the school holidays, and lazing around with the children. Dr Soh and her husband ensure that they are able to bond with their children.

Dr Soh advocates independence for her children, and they will need to learn how to care for themselves and each other when Dad and Mom are not at home. She tries to be an involved parent and supervises closely. At the same time, she always encourages them and motivates them to improve and do better in their studies. Dr Soh feels blessed that she has good, intelligent, open-minded and smart kids.

Apart from her already busy schedule, Dr Soh finds time to participate in meaningful events, including volunteering at nursing homes. As the newly elected President of The Association for Women Doctors (AWDS), she wants to push the recruitment drive to get more women doctors to join their Association. She partakes in the review of the membership privileges and arranges networking events with other women associations.

A smart and beautiful aesthetic doctor with an eye for precision, a mother of four and a fearless businesswoman, Dr Soh definitely fits our criteria of an Extraordinary Woman.

Dr Loretta Chen

Under The Spotlight

My "love story" with Dr Loretta Chen ("Dr Chen") started in early 2013 when I was appointed the sole distributor for George Spyrou's ("George") Daywear and Eveningwear. We wanted to sponsor the eveningwear for a female celebrity with substance and of course with a lovely face and figure. I did some research to find a personality who has both beauty and brains, and Dr Chen fitted the criteria and profile perfectly.

I first met Dr Chen for hi-tea at Shangri-la. I was thinking that I would be meeting with someone who was larger than life and who was condescending because she had achieved so much. Much to my surprise, Dr Chen was a personality who was exceptionally humble, intelligent and beautiful. When Dr Chen agreed that she would be delighted to adorn George's fashion, I sent George her picture and he had the same compliments for this lady of actuality, reality and substance.

After our chichi hi-tea at Shangri-la, Dr Chen was so kind to give me a lift in her car to wherever I was going. We chatted more in the car and I felt much closer to the person whom I will be dressing in George Eveningwear.

George Eveningwear fitted Dr Chen like a glove, both in spirit and in substance, and I was elated to find someone who could bring out the artistry, elegance and style of George's designs so well. I started sponsoring George eveningwear for her events, but had to apologise that there were times when, due to the inventory or timing, I wasn't able to provide the gowns. All she said was, *"Never mind, I will just wear something else"*. I believe if it was someone else, they would have terminated our collaboration. Yet, Dr Chen being Dr Chen, she has the biggest heart to forgive and forget and she continues to wear George Eveningwear which I have been continuing to sponsor for some of her important events.

Our friendship blossomed thanks to George Eveningwear and I got to know more about Dr Chen. Whenever I asked her for help, she would extend her utmost assistance. I remembered that I held a small fashion show at Le Noir and due to the tight budget, I could not employ a renowned host and Dr Chen lent a helping hand by hosting the event at Le Noir. She did not charge me a single cent which I believed would be five-figure if I were to employ her as a host. She also constantly appeared at my pop-up stores to lend me support.

Dr Chen was forever helping me to raise the brand awareness of George's clothes. She would always put up pictures on Facebook, indicating clearly that she was wearing George Eveningwear. From all the assistance and help which I have received from Dr Chen, I felt indebted and I really did not know how to thank her enough. If I could read her mind, she would probably say, "*What are friends for?*"

Not too long ago, I was diagnosed with hyperthyroid and I would get tired very easily. I am not sure if Dr Chen knew about my condition but I remembered I have let her down twice because I have agreed on two occasions to go to the gala events with her but I backed out at the last minute because I was just too tired to go mingle and socialize. I did not ask for forgiveness but if I ever did I perceive that Dr Chen will understand. She would surely say, "*It's ok Karen, I understand*".

Any reader would be able to comprehend from my narration that Dr Chen is a tall lady with a very big heart. Sometimes, I think she is too cordial, gracious and obliging, and thus many have taken advantage of her kindness. If you have read her best-selling memoir entitled *Woman On Top*, you will know what I mean.

It was tough to interview a good friend and especially someone who does interviews and writes exceptionally well. My interview with Dr Chen was candid, uncoloured and unpretentious.

The interview

Q1.   You wear many hats as a successful theatre director, lecturer, DJ with Lush 99.5FM and also the Creative Director for your family's business- VSMD? How do you balance it all?

It is all about passion and having the drive. You must also have a good support network and finding the right balance. As a boss, you should talent-spot and allow your staff to have ownership of their work.

Q2.   Was Theatre your calling or were you influenced by your brother, Edmund Chen, an outstanding Mediacorp Actor?

My eldest brother, Edmund Chen, was definitely a role model. My second brother, Eric, supports my creativity and my parents for allowed me to pursue a career in arts and the theatre.

Q3.   You have recently released your own book which is an instant best-seller with Kinokuniya called *Woman On Top*. Why write a book? Was this what you wanted to do all the time?

I wrote the book to inspire people who are feeling depressed, desperate and who needed an easy-to-read self-help book. When I was doing my doctorate at UCLA, I sunk into depression from the suicide of my girlfriend and her ex-girlfriend. I tried to find self-help books which could elevate me from depression but there was no such book available. So I promised myself that if I got better, I would write a book.

Q4.   If someone aspires to be a creative director or award-winning theatre director, what kind of encouragement would you give to them?

   a.   *Do it for the right reasons;*
   b.   *Surround yourself with positive people;*
   c.   *Be humble yet confident;*
   d.   *Look after yourself;*
   e.   *Travel to broaden your horizons;*
   f.   *Be Observant;*

g.   *Know Thyself and To Thyself Be True;*

h.   *Have a spiritual anchor;*

i.   *Smash the stereotypes; and*

j.   *Break the rules*

(Extracted from Woman On Top)

Q11.   Even in the 21st century, male and female are still unequal, given that many talented and well-educated women have taken a backseat to child rearing after birth and this is expected of them. What do you think about this current state?

We should empower little girls so that they can do it as well if not better than the boys. We should inculcate positive family values whereby boys and girls are treated equally. We should also persuade women to pursue higher education and get their degrees. We should not believe traditional propaganda of what women can and women cannot do.

Q12.   If you are appointed as an NMP, what are the topics that you will look at?

I will look to enhance some of the following:

a.   *Improve the living condition and livelihood of the less fortunate and under-privileged;*

b.   *Do more for the aged;*

c.   *Do more for children with disabilities;*

d.   *Champion for the right of basic education; and*

e.   *Educate the population on how to work with domestic help. Emphasize that domestic help should be treated with respect and dignity.*

Dr Chen is definitely one of my "Extraordinary Woman". She is who she is today because she has gone through so much. She willingly shares with us her ups and downs, her sexuality, her depression, losing a million dollars to a person whom she trusted in a must-read best-selling biography. A remarkable writer, Dr Chen has, in honesty, shared with readers how she emerged from the ashes to a Phoenix. The book **Woman On Top** is on sale at all Kinokuniya outlets. The book is a great inspirational and motivational read.

VI

Ms Marie Choo

The Alchemist and the Avid Dog Rescuer

It was her love for fashion that drove Ms Marie Choo to pursue a career in Fashion. Although she took a diploma in Banking and Finance, she went on to become an Advertising and PR Assistant with Club 21. After a year and a half with Club 21, Ms Choo took her ardent love and passion for fashion to a higher level. She packed her bags and moved to London to pursue a degree in Fashion Product Management. She believed in learning and knowing as much as she could if she had a zealous passion for something.

Upon graduating from Middlesex University, Ms Choo returned to Singapore and joined the FJ Benjamin Group. She climbed the corporate ladder rather quickly and became their Head of Marketing and Communications for their Fashion Division for 4 years before she decided to take a break.

Being in the corporate world for a long time, it was just very natural for Ms Choo to feel restless after a short time and being the workaholic she was, she started her own PR Company called Alchemy Consultancy. Ms Choo put in a lot of effort and worked long and arduous hours during the first few years of the inception of the company, but she was blessed with top brands which placed their trust in her.

Ms Choo started off with clients from the LVMH group, namely Thomas Pink, Moet & Chandon, Dom Perignon, Krug, Hennessy, Belvedere, Cloudy Bay and Cape Mentelle. It has been seven years since Ms Choo started Alchemy Consultancy in January 2008, and she is very charmed to still count the prominent brands such as G.H.Mumm, Perrier-Jouet, Gaggenau, Schott Zwiesel as her key accounts.

At the initial start of her PR Company, Ms Choo suffered a heavy setback by partnering with the wrong person and because she did not think that a partnership agreement was required, things went awry. She had to pay a substantial amount of money to buy out the shares which her ex-partner held. This episode made her more wary about contractual terms and the need for contracts to be in place being in the business.

I met Ms Choo once when I was starting my own business. She was prim and proper, dressed-to-the nines while I was a frumpy mother who had just given birth to a 3.75kg baby. What's more, I did not even cover my grey hairs and I felt so flustered sitting beside such a charmer. Ms Choo was poised and offered to buy me a cup of coffee. I could not remember what our discussion was about but I could vividly remember that she warned me to be careful about distributing proposals because someone might just take your ideas and make it theirs. From a very experienced marketing communications and PR specialist, I heeded her golden words and I protected myself by becoming more alert and cautious about sending out drafted proposals.

Besides being the owner of a PR company, Ms Choo's other full-time job is being the founder and driver of the Dogs Owners Guidance Support (D.O.G.S). D.O.G.S (Singapore) Limited which is a registered charity under the Charities Act. The charity organisation's mission is to be a voice for the dogs, to assist various dogs' welfare groups, independent dog rescuers, and help dog owners.

The dog charity is also focused on public awareness programs on dog ownership, good canine behaviour, preparing and providing volunteers and fosterers with the right knowledge to help dogs. The charity also provided complimentary rehabilitation sessions for dogs to overcome their issues which made them more adoptable. The ultimate goal of D.O.G.S is to help rehome rescued dogs, impart knowledge to owners to ensure that they have a meaningful relationship with their dogs, try to reduce dog abuse and abandonment and other dog related issues.

Ms Choo's craving for learning about a subject she is very keen on is insatiable. She even took a degree in Canine Behaviour and Training so that she is equipped with more knowledge on canine behavior and how to rescue dogs using the correct methodology. Ms Choo's love for dogs started at a young age. She always had a dog as a pet during her growing years. However, the eventual turning point for her was Butter, the Shetland Sheepdog that came into Ms Choo's life in 2010. Butter had a great influence on Ms Choo and even inspired her to volunteer in dog welfare, start a dog charity and even pursue a degree in Canine Behaviour and Training.

She said, "*I was born to love dogs.*" To her, dogs are very inspiring creatures. I could not agree more because a dog's loyalty, unconditional love and faith for their owners are sterling virtues for humanity to learn from.

Ms Choo's passion in making D.O.G.S a success derived from seeing the dogs that they had rescued dogs go to great homes and living a good life, away from battering and abuse. Some of the most touching moments which Ms Choo had, were when new owners of the rescued dogs sent her pictures of the rescued dogs looking happy and well-taken of. To Ms Choo, all the rescue dogs that came into her life were very much like her own children. She knew each of them by names, their temperament and she endeavoured to stay in touch with the new families the rescued dogs were placed with. Ms Choo remained very concerned about how they were doing after they were being placed with their new owners.

Apart from running D.O.G.S, Ms Choo is also a dog behaviourist and trainer who use positive reinforcement techniques to convert a dog's undesired and ill-favoured behaviourial patterns into desired and coveted behaviourial patterns. In 2012, Ms Choo started to train dogs officially at the shelters where she volunteered whereby she assisted to modify and reform the behaviour of the rescued dogs. She has completed her module in Understanding Canine Care & Behaviour from The Cambridge Institute of Dog Behaviour and Training and she is now in the midst of completing her second module in Common Canine Behaviour Problems. She is trying hard to complete her modules and crossing the hurdles necessary so that she can pursue her degree in Canine Behaviour and Training with the Middlesex University in the United Kingdom.

Ms Choo retraced the strict protocols that D.O.G.S takes when it comes to an intervention and rescue.

The first step is to send to the vet for a basic check-up because the charity would need to know the general health of the dog and if it had any contagious diseases before they were sent it to a foster home or had the dog rehomed. It was only responsible and proper for the charity to inform the potential family about the possible financial and time commitment when it comes to adopting a dog with any illnesses.

The second step is to assess the temperament of the dog. Besides running her own PR agency, Marie is also practicing as a dog behaviourist and trainer. Hence, that is why she is also responsible for the most of the hands-on work with the dogs which D.O.G.S rescues and handles. Once she determines the temperament of the dog, it is much easier for the charity to match the dog to the right family.

The third step is to create awareness for the dog on D.O.G.S Facebook page. This is also how the charity looks for potential fosterers and adopters.

The final step is that once the dog charity finds a potential fosterer or adopter, the next thing to do is for a home visit as the charity needs to ascertain that the environment is conducive for the dog's well-being. At the same time, it is also an opportunity for Marie and her team to advise the fosterer or adopter about basic dog training and behaviour.

With so much on her plate, Marie still makes time for her husband of nine years. They are still very much in love and would go for daily walks with their dogs and go on dates at any time of the week. This Valentine's day was special for them because the couple spent it with a good friend whose husband was overseas. Another meaning of Valentine's Day is also Friendship Day and Marie had the best of both worlds this Valentine's Day.

VII

Ms Tan Kheng Hua

An Actress Of Steel

Ms Tan Kheng Hua is one of the most prolific and popular actresses in Singapore. She shot to fame with her role as Margaret Phua in Mediacorp's longest running television comedy sitcom **Phua Chu Kang Pte Ltd.**

The interview with Ms Tan was candid, straightforward and with many learning points. As we want to credit, commend and acknowledge the entire interview to one of the most down-to-earth, no-nonsense and realistic actresses, we have decided to keep the interview intact and in its entirety.

The interview

Q1.   After graduating from University, you worked in marketing first. Were you afraid to make a foray into acting or did your parents want you to work in the corporate world first and then make a decision later?

Neither. After graduating, going into acting full-time was never in my consciousness! A full-time English speaking actor in Singapore in the early 1980s? Was there even such a thing? I didn't know any part-time actors much less full-time actors. I took a marketing job because I was interested in it, studied it at school, found that I could do it reasonably well and because someone actually thought I was good enough to join their company! My parents are very lenient. They'd let me do whatever I wanted.

Q2.   The first stage play which you acted in was The Waiting Room by John Bowen and produced by Ivan Heng? How did you feel about your first stage play? Were you nervous?

I felt very excited, very nervous, very in love with the theatre, very hooked on acting and very indebted to the person who gave me that opportunity in the first place — my cousin, Ivan Heng! He's still one of my heroes today.

Q3.   Was your family supportive of your decision to go into acting?

After many years of working full-time and spending every other moment outside of work in the theatre, I told my parents I wanted to quit my full-time employ and I still remember what my mum said, "Good. Good. Now you will have more time to go on holidays with us".

Q4. You took about 10 years to move into full-time acting. Why did you take one decade to move into acting full-time?

The short answer to that is that I really enjoyed my full-time work — doing public affairs, marketing services and PR for C K Tang Pte Ltd. I had a great boss, Gerry Rezel and great colleagues and everyday was really a joy there. And every moment after work running into the theatre and being obsessed till way past midnight and then having supper and then sleeping late and waking up again to go to work and having that cycle start all over again was...HEAVEN! I call those the GLORIOUS DAYS! So in love with what I was discovering about life, myself. It was intoxicating and therefore I didn't feel the urge to change it for a long time. I could cope. I did well in both my corporate as well as my artistic life. It was only after I got married, bought a house and felt more emotionally secure after Yu-Beng came into my life that I seriously thought about changing it in a big way. And with his support, and a bank account that benefitted from someone never spending any money I earned because rather than be in the clubs, I was in the theatre, I did!

Q5. You are one of Singapore's most popular actresses and best known for your role as *Margaret Phua* in MediaCorp's longest-running English language hit television sitcom *Phua Chu Kang Pte Ltd*. Did you like the sitcom itself? Do you think it was your best performance? Were all of you like a real family after working together for so long?

I didn't like the sitcom. I loved it. At first. And then after awhile, I may not have loved it as much, but I loved being IN it, because going to work and hanging with the PCK family was a hoot everyday. We were uncontrollably mischievous and spent most of our time laughing and doing stupid things and playing games rather than rehearsing. I still miss that and miss them and we keep in touch with a very silly whatsapp chat group. No, it was not my best performance. I am at heart, a drama actress and by no means a comedian. But acting with very funny people like Gurmit and Sweenie helped loads.

Q6.   Since 2000, you became a producer and produced critically acclaimed box-office hits like "*Revenge of the Dim Sum Dollies*", "*Dim Sum Dollies – Singapore's Most Wanted!*" and "*Dim Sum Dollies in Little Shop of Horrors*". In addition, you were also named the best actress by DBS Life! in 2002 and Art Nation in 2003. What are your thoughts about achieving so much in your acting career?

Honestly, there are days I wake up and I feel as if I haven't achieved a lot. Then there are days I wake up and I feel really proud of what I have done. There are days I wake up and I feel I want everyone to know how much I have achieved, and then there are days I wake up and I think, "My God, Kheng, get off your high horse and give something back." Most of the days, I don't think about achievements at all. Wouldn't you say I am like the next person when it comes to perceptions about "achievements in life".

Q7.   You are married to another successful actor Mr Lim Yu Beng since 1996. Was it difficult to be married to a fellow actor? Was it a competing relationship or was a complimentary relationship? (I just wanted to know if you competed in your acting careers or was it a complimentary relationship whereby you discuss about your acting gigs or stage productions and provide each other with support and advice?)

I wouldn't say Yubes (that's why Yu-Beng is commonly known as by people close to him) and my relationship is competitive or complimentary. Our approaches to work and life are often very different, and that has sometimes made talking about our "shared" passion difficult. Having said that though, there are areas in our relationship where our simpatico and agreement is unbelievably aligned. Our love for our daughter, for instance, and how the both of us are so often in agreement as to how to raise her, even without any in depth discussion. And she has joined the triumvirate because she is in the School Of The Arts — and in handling her emerging artistic streak, both Yubes and I have also found how aligned we are in many artistic, and philosophical perceptions. Having said all this, we are now currently working together as producer, me, and writer/director, Yubes, for a theatre project in Penang called 2 Houses and so far, things have run rather smoothly. I think old age, greater tolerance and a growing distaste for dissention as well as understanding that it's not THAT important to have it your way, helps a great deal. Oh, and we've been married since 1992.

Q8.   What was your first reaction when you knew you were going to be a mommy?

Pure joy. No other time have I experienced pure joy like that moment.

Q9.   Were you prepared for your pregnancy?

I never prepared consciously for my pregnancy. But pregnancy and motherhood are two of the most natural things for me. I never felt a need to work so hard at it, like "prepare" etc. Many other things I struggle with, but not pregnancy and motherhood.

Q10.   Was your husband supportive during the pregnancy?

Extremely.

Q11.   Were you prepared for your own childbirth?

Shi-An is my first child, I think no matter how hard you prepare, you can't really. As much as I think preparing is important, I have also seen people prepare TOO much, think they can control their childbirth too much. And that's not good too.

Q12.　　How have things changed since you have become a mother?

Wow. This is a difficult question. My first instinct is to say everything has changed. But on second thought, it's more like, everything is enhanced more than changed. Life, love, joy, sadness, anger, frustration, my work, my free time, my relationship with my own mother, relationship with Yu-Beng, even my relationship with close friends and my brothers, the tones of these feelings or relationships are enhanced in one way or the other, good and bad. And the reason for this is because of the deep, unquestioning, unconditional love for her.

The best thing that has changed since I became a mother is probably that of all the sides of Kheng, I like myself as a mother most of all. She brings out the best things in me. And I am very thankful that the one person I love most in this world does that for me. It would be tragic if the one person you love most in the world brings out the worst in you. I have seen that happen. It's not pretty.

Q13.　　Did you take time off from your career during your daughter's early childhood years to spend more time with her and bond with her?

Even until today, I am very protective of my time with her. I love to be with her! We have a good time. I don't do it because I need to "bond" with her. I do it because she's really fun to be with! People think that parents setting aside special time to be with their children is for the child's sake. I would like to introduce the notion that it is very much for the parents' sake as well. Without my time with Shi-An, I am not as steady. That's how it is with a good love. You need each other to get the day going good, for our hearts to build the right muscles to tend to the things we need to tend to.

Q14. You have an extremely tough working schedule as a stage and television producer, so how do you manage your schedule and spend enough time with your daughter?

Easy. Just decide and do it. Commit to it. Commit to this schedule, this amount of sleep, this chore, this holiday, this work problem to solve, this activity with your child, this trip to the supermarket, this trip to the vet, this phone call to your mum, and then just do it. Follow through the best you can. Try to be good natured while you're doing it by reminding yourself that you want ALL these things in your life and if you WANT all these things in your life, well then, you just got to go out and do it and don't complain. And if you don't feel like doing ALL these things for awhile, that's possible too. Decide and do.

Q15. As a mother, what do you expect from your daughter?

I want her to do enjoy life. Discover and then hone some skills that will allow her to find her place in the world in a joyous and effective way. I want her to love and be loved on terms that will make her and her partner happy and fulfilled. I want her to know that I am there if she needs a chat anytime she wavers. A Chat, rather than a Lecture as to what to do. I want her to know nothing is insurmountable and that she is not alone. I want her to know the highs and lows of human nature, to try not to judge and that she has the option to choose the way to be and the sort of life to live.

Q16. What type of education or values do you want to inculcate or have inculcated in your daughter?

Honestly, Yubes and I have left her education pretty much to her. We haven't helped her in her homework since she was 9. And not very effectively before that even. We don't take parent-teacher meets too seriously because honestly, we don't think her teachers can tell us anything about our daughter we don't know better. We don't really know when her exams are and we leave her to do what she feels needs to be done. She sets her own schedules, chooses her own subjects, decides whether she wants tuition or not and whether she needs to buckle down and mug or have some time out and play for a bit so she can buckle down later. We're there, as people to take care of her, love her, give her the emotional support so she knows if she doesn't fulfill her own expectations, it's going to be okay. But when it comes to studies, exams, what sort of curriculum, how much to study etc, we've always left it pretty much to her.

Q17.   Are you satisfied with your daughter's current school curriculum?

I don't know much about it really, even though it's SOTA and I am in performing arts. My role there is as Shi-An's mum. Not an actress. Not a producer. Not her teachers' friend.

Q18.   How do you bond with your daughter?

I am lucky in that I can live everyday life with my daughter without consciously having to plan "bonding" sessions, which can be a bore and very contrived. What is very naturally bonding is sharing similar interests and finding comfort in the same things. For example, Shi-An and I love to potter about at home rather than fight crowds in a mall. I love to cook, and she loves my food. We love to watch movies on her computer. We have the same taste in what clothes we think suits us and each other, which does not mean we have the same taste. I like her friends and her friends feel comfortable with me and that makes it easy for her to bring her teen world into the one she shares with me. That's very important, being able to share the different parts of your daughter's world (because honestly, you can't and don't want to be the be all and end all of your children's lives) so that she can share parts of her that does not include you WHEN and IF she feels like it. Children should have that privilege and privacy, because they need to learn to be their own people and if you're meddling all the time, they'll never learn that. And if you're judging and telling all the time, they'll keep away from you.

Q19.   Do you mind if your daughter takes up acting as a full-time career?

Of course not!

Q20.   What is the latest family activity or family trip that you have taken with your family?

We all went skiing in Europe at the end of last year. It is a yearly affair and has been for the last 11 years. We love it.

Q21.   What are the recent projects that you have done?

I was shooting The Empress Dowager in the new Netflix mini-series Marco Polo in Johore from May 2014. On top of my acting engagement, I was also helping out with The O.P.E.N., the public engagement initiative of The Singapore International Festival of Arts 2014 and producing a big project call THE SIN-PEN COLONY for The Georgetown Festival 2014, a series of four projects celebrating the shared heritage of Penang and Singapore.

Q22.   What kind of advice do you have for mothers who are struggling with their career and family?

Gosh, I don't know if I believe in giving general advice because what helps one can be totally detrimental for another. If you ask me what has helped me when I felt a struggle between career and family, I'd say — decide what you want from both aspects of your life, decide who is affected by those decisions and take their well-being into consideration, decide on an action towards those goals, and then do it the best you can and minimize the guilt. Guilt can be very detrimental, degenerative and counter-productive.

Beyond a shadow of doubt, I enjoyed my interview with Kheng Hua. I thought to myself I could not have met someone more gracious. After many arrangements and when we could not meet, Kheng Hua was kind enough to pen out the whole interview via email. All I can say is that I am grateful to her and I have learnt so much about the passion for acting and parenting from an amiable, engaging and friendly artiste.

VIII

Ms Wong Li Lin

The Dance Of My Life

I was extremely delighted when Ms Wong Li-Lin ("Li-Lin) decided to have "a-go" at my interview. To be honest, her career has been a delight to watch. After graduating from the Royal Ballet School in the UK, she decided that she was not going to dance professionally but engaged herself with acting, fitness and even pioneered Pilates in Singapore.

I always felt that we had something in common and that was classical ballet. I was trained in classical ballet by Mdm Lim Beng

Soon for 9 years before I switched to train with Mrs Hung Yee Skipp for one year. I loved dancing but I did not have much family support. I liked ballet but I never thought I danced well.

It was even more remorseful when you did not have much support because every parent at my age hoped that their children would become a doctor, lawyer or accountant not a ballet dancer. However, my training in ballet gave me my poise and made a more creative person. After dancing for 10 years, I finally gave in to my parents to stop dancing and concentrate on my studies. It was rather regrettable that I did not complete my ballet studies because of ballet, I felt free. Now, I dance every time before my children and they will dance with me too.

I believe that Ms Wong who had completed her ballet training would have felt the same. Ballet gave her strength, poise, grace, creativity, fitness and freedom. No sport in the world would be able to give you what classical ballet could.

"If anything at all, perfection is not when there is nothing to add, but when there is nothing left to take away." quoted from Maria Tallchief. Ballet is perfection and it is the only vocation that creates a sculpture that is only visible for a moment in time.

The interview

Q1.   I understand you have been placed in several foster homes when you were a child before living with your ballet teacher, Ms Hung Yee Skipp at the age of fourteen. Has living in foster care and later with your ballet teacher, Ms Hung Yee Skipp, made you a much stronger and resilient person? Were you affected by so many changes at a young age?

All our experiences in life would have an impact on us. I had the good fortune of being exposed to the colorful spectrums that make up life and human behavior. I love it. Of course as a child it might have been confusing and many times painful. And you deal with it the best you can... as might be a situation with life as an adult too. What is helpful is if we don't use our conditions or the external factors of our life as a determination of what we are and who we are. It is extremely important to connect with ourselves to see what we want to create. We can design the lives we want. That power lies in our hands solely.

Q2.   Are you estranged from your own family? Do you still keep in touch with them?

No, I am not estranged from my family. And yes I see them, speak to them, eat with them as most of us might with our families.

Q3.   You won the prestigious Loke Cheng Kim scholarship to study ballet at Royal Ballet School in the United Kingdom (UK), was this opportunity a life-changer for you?

Yes of course. To live in England and to train at one of the top institutions in the world, with some of the most brilliant dancers ever no less... was a dream come true.

Q4.   You studied ballet from a young age, did you dance professionally?

I actually started late at age 9. I realized I love the art. And that passion can be manifested in many creative and helpful ways. Dancing professionally was not one of the ways I wanted to pursue. Ballet — being on stage, being near the stage, being with dancers, looking at Instagram accounts of dancers — they excite me and bring me such a joy that I can only say that it is in my blood and whatever I do, I am a ballet dancer foremost.

Q5.   You have been trained in ballet for a long time. Most ballerinas want to have a svelte physique and there are so any stories about ballerinas dealing with bouts of anorexia or bulimia so as to keep their thin-frame. Did you experience such medical conditions before?

No.

Q6.   What made you decide to become an actress and a host?

It was by accident. I was teaching at the TV station when they asked me to play a part on TV.

Q7.   You made your television debut in 1994 and acted in dramas such as *Masters of the Sea, Rising Expectation* and became a household name when you acted as Inspector Elaine Tay in Mediacorp's Channel 5 cop drama series, *Triple Nine* from 1995 to 1997. After a brief hiatus from acting, you returned to small screen and acted frequently in Channel 8 dramas like *Love Me, Love Me Not, The Challenge* and *The Reunion*. In 2008, you starred in Singapore's romantic movie, *The Leap Years*, and gained more popularity. You were nominated as the Best Performer in the Singapore Film Awards in 2009 for the movie *The Leap Years*. Besides acting, you were also a judge for the reality TV series *The Dance Floor*. With so many years of acting, dancing and hosting experience, which job was your favourite?

I made my debut in a Christmas special called Silent Night. *I don't really have a favourite per se and that is because I think they are all there for good reason. I can say that I feel most intimately connected with dance. It was the kernel to everything else that sprouted from there, including acting and hosting.*

Q8.   If you have the chance to change your career, would you still want to be an actress and host?

If the option is there. I have chosen not to be a full time actress and host.

Q9.   Your love for dancing and fitness created a Singapore movement for Pilates. How long were you trained in Pilates and why did you bring Pilates to Singapore?

I pioneered Pilates in Singapore. I was trained while at the Royal Ballet and then subsequently went to the US to train with the last disciple of Pilates, Eve Gentry as well as her prodigee Michele Larson. When I first tried Pilates I felt instinctively that this would be the future and that it would be helpful for many.

Q10.   We were all quite surprised when you decided uproot and move to Shanghai with your family. Why did you move to Shanghai? Were there more work opportunities in Shanghai? Did you like Shanghai?

We moved to Shanghai because my ex-husband wanted to explore opportunities there. I was not there for work. Yes I like Shanghai – it is an extremely dynamic place, love the architecture of the older quarters and I really appreciated the physical link to the ancestry that is me as an ethnic Chinese.

Q11.   I understand that you were a stay-at-home mom for nine years after your marriage and now that you are working full-time, do you miss spending quality time with your children?

I still spend quality time with my kids. They are in school most of the day as I am at work.

Q12. You created Loopz Fitness, you are consulting for Parkway Pantai Group and also working in a company that manages high-net worth individuals. How do you manage your time with 3 jobs and taking care of your family?

I have left the high net worth group now to focus on my work with wellness and also media.

Q13. It seems like a light-year ago, but what was your first reaction when you knew you were going to be a mommy?

Surprise.

Q14. Were you prepared for your pregnancy?

After the initial surprise, yes. I was very excited.

Q15. Was your ex-husband supportive during the pregnancy?

Yes as much as he could be.

Q16. Were you prepared for your own childbirth?

Yes.

Q17. How have things changed since you have become a mother?

Everything has changed. I am sure all parents feel the same way.

Q18. What moral values do you want to instill in your children?

My key responsibility is to provide them with the tools to the amazing resources that they already possess. We talk a lot about love and respect, and honoring these values. Being centered so our words, thoughts and actions might be clear. Moreover, we alone have the power and ability to design the lives we want.

Q19.   How do you cope with the high-profile divorce from fellow media artiste, Allan Wu? Was the divorce mutual?

Yes.

Q20.   How did you relate to your children that "daddy and mommy" are no longer going to stay together? Did the divorce make them stronger and more understanding?

Mom and Dad will always be their Mom and Dad. That doesn't change.

Q21.   Are you satisfied with your children's current school curriculum?

It is not a concern for me. The world is a school, not just the physical premise they visit from Monday to Friday.

Q22.   Would you be jumping onto the dating wagon anytime soon?

I have no qualms meeting people, going on dates. But I am emphatic that I have zero interest in anything serious at the moment. This is MY time to build me.

Q23.   What is the latest family activity or family trip that you have taken with your family?

The kids and I were in Bali last year. I think it will be Malaysia in CNY next.

Q24.   What kind of advice do you have for mothers who are struggling with their career and family?

One foot in front of the other. Don't make it a struggle, instead make what you can do to create what you want. The power is in you, not what is happening external of you.

Besides being a dancer, fitness pioneer, actress and a host, Ms Wong already has so much on her plate. Above all, she is also a very protective mother to her 10-year-old daughter Sage and 9-year old son Jonas. With her amazing strength and positivity, Ms Wong's story is one that inspires and motivates. She has shown us that even though the road in front of you may seem trudging and tough, you create your own life with the power within yourself.

IX

Ms Xiang Yun

Singapore's Evergreen Actress

"*The Awakening*". How these words aptly describe my feelings as I strode into MediaCorp with the enticing prospect of speaking to my childhood idol, and how apt the words to introduce the lovely lady who so amicably accommodated to my request for an interview. Despite her unforgiving busy schedule, Xiang Yun arranged some time off to speak to me. I was so excited that I am finally going to have a real "*heart-to-heart conversation*" with Xiang Yun!

I remembered when Xiang Yun's whole family moved to my parents' neighbourhood when I was a youthful adolescent. Although I was too young to appreciate the essence of the Chinese drama series then, I was captivated by Xiang Yun's persona and I was always trying to garner courage to go up to Xiang Yun and say "Hi, how are you doing today and can I have an autograph?"

Embarking on my current book project, it was imperative for me to include Xiang Yun, one of Singapore's most iconic actresses whose acting career spans more than three decades, as one of my interviewees.

My first impression of Xiang Yun was that she looked the same as she was when I saw her in my teens, not a day older! In her smart casual attire, she greeted me with such warmth and friendliness that it felt like she was my best friend in school and we had lost touch for a long time before meeting up again (since Facebook was not invented then).

Although I was frantically writing down the interview notes, Xiang Yun made me feel like I was having a tea-time conversation and not a serious interview. With all her accomplishment, she was very down-to-earth, friendly and certainly likeable, just like on television. No doubt why she was one of the "Top 10 Most Popular Artistes" in the annual Star Awards for a decade no less. After winning the coveted "Top 10 Most Popular Artistes" Award, Xiang Yun went on to win the "All-Time Favourite Artiste" Award in 2011.

Xiang Yun started off her career with Rediffusion at the tender age of 12 years. It was at Redifussion that she learned her Mandarin and cultivated her interest towards the Chinese Language. When Xiang Yun graduated from secondary school, she joined Singapore Broadcasting Station's Drama Class and began her exciting career in acting. Xiang Yun mentioned that she owed part of her success to her father, a taxi-driver who dedicated his time ferrying his daughter to and from Reddifusion.

In the 1980s, Xiang Yun propelled to fame for her character as "Ah Mei" where she acted as the love interest Huang Wenyong's character as "Ah Shui" in the epic drama *The Awakening*. When I asked Xiang Yun how she handled the stress that came with fame and popularity at a young age, she answered that the only thing different was that she was getting more acting roles, audience and much busier than before. Xiang Yun commented that the pioneer generation of actors and actresses rarely thought of themselves as celebrities. Mostly felt that acting was a passion and a job.

Not long after Xiang Yun shot to fame, she fell in love with SBC's charismatic actor, Edmund Chen. After a whirlwind courtship, they registered for marriage. Their immense love and respect for each other was real and true. Their courtship and subsequent marriage became a hot topic for all media at that time. True to their vows, after two decades of marriage, Edmund Chen and Xiang Yun are still in love and happily married with two beautiful children.

When Xiang Yun became pregnant with her first child, she was unable to take up any acting roles. Hence, MediaCorp posted her to work as a voice-over artist. Xiang Yun commented that she was worried that the transfer would be permanent and she would not be able to pursue her favourite vocation as an actress.

As a first-time mother, Xiang Yun had her own anxieties. Her husband, Edmund Chen, was not around most of the time as he was busy recording his music albums in China. To date, Edmund had recorded and released 5 music albums. With so much on his own plate, Edmund was not always able to help out with the caring of their first child. Xiang Yun mentioned that there was an incident which caused her to be terribly exhausted and upset. She related she was fraught and fatigued when both Edmund and her baby son had chickenpox at the same time. This is a stark example of the trials and tribulations of motherhood.

Although Xiang Yun was under an absolute amount of stress as a new mother, her son brought her immense happiness. In good time, Xiang Yun left her voice-over artist position and returned to acting full-time. Nearly a decade later, Xiang Yun gave birth to her beautiful daughter at the age of 40 years old. This time, she was well-prepared for child-birth and was thus more confident in the caring of her daughter.

As a parent, Xiang Yun gives her children the freedom to do what they want, but she stressed that they must take their education seriously. Xiang Yun and Edmund Chen also share their life experiences with their children and by doing so, they are able to build a very strong bond with their children. Their son, Yixi, is now in Nanyang Technological University finishing his degree and their daughter, Yixin, is in secondary school.

As a mother of a grown-up university student and a teenager, Xiang Yun chooses her work projects thoughtfully so that she is able to manage her time carefully between work projects and her family. Xiang Yun wants to focus and give it all when she is working on a drama, film or stage project. Furthermore, Xiang Yun also has her hands full with her endorsement projects and thus she is extremely meticulous when it comes to time management. Upon completion of her work projects, Xiang Yun wants to be able to spend quality time with her husband, Edmund Chen and their 2 children. Therefore, no matter how difficult the situation is, Xiang Yun always manages to engage attentively and put her best foot forward with her work projects and when she is with her family, she is also able to dedicate her full attention and spend quality time with her family. This is an explicit and true account of how a working mom conscientiously tries to balance her limited amount of time between her career and family life and Xiang Yun makes it seem so easy!

When we discussed about Edmund Chen, Xiang Yun reveals that Edmund is an introvert. He loves to travel and paint. He often rallies the whole family to plan for travel trips. Everyone in the family has to get involved with the planning of the trip, which is great for family bonding!

Beyond shadow of doubt, Xiang Yun is one of the most easy-going, delightful and warm celebrities that I have met. She is not only an award-winning actress, but a wonderful wife and a remarkable mother to her children. To have a career and a good family comes only with setting your priorities right. I believe Xiang Yun has every right to be proud of herself for managing and balancing both her career and family life so well. She sets an admirable example for women who are struggling with work-life balance in our competitive and dynamic society.

Ms Yap Shu Mei

My Happiness Is Playing My Violin

I met Ms Yap Shu Mei when my first son was playing violin with an ensemble of young children. I saw how Ms Yap was teaching the class effectively and everyone in her class seemed to enjoy her lessons. With a very strong and graceful presence, Ms Yap caught my attention immediately. In fact, my son, Caden, was vehement about changing to Ms Yap's solo class. He said that he wanted to be taught by a pretty teacher. Unfortunately, Ms Yap's teaching time was limited and she was not able to teach Caden.

In all seriousness, Ms Yap made teaching a class of at least 15 young children look so simple. As I relish in interviewing women from different backgrounds for my website and my book, **Extraordinary Women – Singapore**, Ms Yap seems to shine through. I emailed her and asked her if I was able to interview her and she was quick to respond positively. I was elated that she could do the interview. Hence, I drafted the questions and emailed it to her and the rest was history.

"*Life is like playing a violin solo in public and learning the instrument as one goes on.*" said Samuel Butler.

The interview

Q1.   Why did you choose music as a career?

   Since I was in secondary school, I decided that I wanted to do Music or Medicine. My intention to do medicine was because I wanted to be a missionary doctor like Dr Albert Schweitzer. As a matter of fact, I thought I could be a good gynaecologist. My love for music is pure and untainted.

   I attended my Cambridge "A" Level classes at Raffles Junior College. I did biology as part of my curriculum. One serene afternoon, when we were all dissecting a rat in the biology lab, I looked around me and saw that all my classmates were so absorbed in the dissection of their rats and looking attentively into their microscope. All at once, it dawned onto me that there were so many of them who wanted to be doctors but there were not many who crave the career of being a professional violinist.

I thought deeply about being a physician and being a violinist. I discussed intensively with my then violin teacher, Ms Vivien Goh on the prospects of being a violinist. I also asked her if Singapore needed more violin teachers. Her answer was a clear YES. It was then and there that I decided to pursue my music degree overseas. I sought her help to recommend me to the best tertiary music schools in the United States of America (USA). Ms Goh also helped me to prepare for the entrance audition.

Q2.   Did your parents encourage you to pursue music as your career?

No. Like most parents of my generation, my parents wanted their children to do medicine or law. For my parents, they hoped that I would become a doctor because of our church influence. They like my sisters and me to play music but not to make a career out of it.

Q3.   Why did you become to become a violinist when you can pursue other music vocations?

Violin was the only instrument I took lessons in and was proficient at it. Furthermore, Singapore indeed needed more violin teachers as confirmed by my violin teacher, Ms Vivien Goh.

Q4.   When did you start your formal music education?

I started formal violin lessons when I was eight years old. Before that, I was fiddling with whatever instruments there were such as the piano, pianica, guitar and harmonica. In fact, I performed quite a bit on the harmonica for the church as a child and my performances were always well-received.

One day, I had a chance to watch the musical "Fiddler on the Roof". I was captivated by the Orchestra, mainly the string instruments. I could not get enough of it and when I got home, I used a stick and started bowing on the guitar and pretended that the guitar was my cello. My eldest sister was so fascinated and amused that she encouraged my mother to let me learn the violin.

Q5.   Besides violin, do you play many other instruments professionally?

No. I could play the piano but I was not formally trained in it. I also tried playing the guitar and drums as an adult but again I am not good at those instruments.

Q6.   You are a highly sought-after performance violinist and masterclass clinician for violin studies. Do you prefer performing or teaching?

I enjoy a good balance of both.

Q7.   Did you establish Mandeville Conservatory of Music?

Yes. I established the Music Conservatory 19 years ago after I came back from my London post-graduate studies. I started the music school together with an ex-colleague Ken Tan from Singapore Symphony Orchestra (SSO).

Q8.   Why did you decide to start a music school?

I was teaching privately from home and in La Salle College then. I wanted a place where I could run through my music curriculum and share ideas with many more colleagues.

Q9.   I understand that Mandeville Conservatory of Music has been around for 19 years and produced many accredited and talented musicians. How do you feel achieving so much as a teacher, performer and jazz violinist besides being a very successful businesswoman with Mandevillle Conversatory of Music?

As a teacher, I am satisfied when my students continue to play music for life whether they make a career out of it or not. My teaching philosophy is to teach every child to love music and to use music to communicate in a useful way.

As a jazz violinist, I am proud to be one of very few here in Singapore who can improvise on the violin and playing in jazz clubs and concerts. In addition, I am absolutely honoured of having produced two CDs. My first CD called, "Jazz Canvas-Asian Memories", was released in June 2000 with 5 original compositions and 5 re-arrangements of Asian children folk tunes.

My 2nd CD has just been released in September 2014 with 15 original Christian songs written by me. I produced it together with my jazz violin mentor Christian Howes. The CD was a compilation of a jazz gospel featuring jazz violin played Christian and myself. The lead singer for the CD was Ms Jenika Marion, a young, beautiful and versatile singer from the USA. Ms Marina Xavier, a renowned local pop and soul sensation also collaborated with us on the CD including two other American singers."

As a businesswoman, I am proud that my school has become one of the most established music schools in Singapore and one with the most number of violin students. I am also very proud to be the Founder and Program Director of the Singapore International String Conference since 2002.

Q10.   You also teach baby violin, how do you bond with the young children in your classes?

I enjoy teaching kids 3-5 years old. This has become a passion for me because I will be their first teacher to introduce the wonderful instrument, violin, to them. For students from Baby Violin course, I have a clean piece of paper to start my drawing on. I am able to mould and influence younger children more ably and competently. On top of this, I also encourage and teach parents to bond with their kids through playing the violin together. In this way, parents and children are able to bond effectively and nurture their love for violin together. For young children, I teach them violin by using effectual games and with a lot of singing in class.

Q11. What advice would you give to parents who want their children to further their studies in music?

Parents should let their children do what they desire to do. Parents should love them deeply and encourage them to pursue their desires with passion. They should guide them in the right paths and help them focus on their paths.

Q12. You encourage using technology to advance music teaching, why is this so?

I have to use technology simply to keep up with times.

Q13. What is the peculiar difference between playing an acoustic violin versus an electric violin?

The sound comes from different sources. For acoustic, it comes from the violin itself but for electric violin; the sound comes from a sound system which it is plug into such as an amplifier, a monitor or ear monitors.

Q14. Will you be performing with Singapore Symphony of Music in 2015? Do you have any performance dates planned?

I played with the SSO from 1990-1993 and have not played with them since then. Now I prefer to play jazz violin because of the creative element it offers. I have just performed a few

Christmas gigs. The next performance will be the 8th Feb 2015 for my CD launch at the Singapore Art Museum.

Q15.   Besides music, what are your other interests?

I have been scuba diving since 1992. I take about three to four scuba diving trips a year. I enjoy cycling and walking my dog. I enjoy food, especially good authentic Japanese food. Like most women, I adore shopping and pampering myself in the spa. I have also become the ambassador of the ClearSK Aesthetic Clinics.

Q16.   Do you prefer to play the classical violin or the electric violin? And why?

I enjoy playing both. The situation calls for the right instrument. If I play chamber music, classical music, in acoustic settings or recording studios that do not require amplification, then I prefer to play an acoustic violin. There are more colours and nuance that can be coaxed out of a good and responsive acoustic violin.

I will use electric violin when I have to play contemporary music like jazz, pop and rock music with a band which uses instruments that are all amplified electronically. The acoustic violin, when amplified, tend to sound shrill and could have feedback issues when the instrument is over-amplified.

Q17.   You are a prolific violinist, a much sought-after violin teacher, a jazz musician, businesswoman and a keen scuba diver, how do you balance and have it all? Do you have any personal time at all?

I have plenty of personal time and I plan it this way. I take short holidays almost every month to rejuvenate myself.

The secret is that I do not require a lot of sleep. I can sleep 4-5 hours a day and that is quite enough for me. If I sleep too much, I will get a headache! I believe I manage my time well because every morning I pray and ask God to lengthen my days, to give me wisdom and to guide me in all that I do.

XI

Ms Zoe Tay

Queen Of Caldecott Hill

She is the irrefutable extraordinaire, *Queen of Caldecott Hill.*

A prime example of poise, refinement and beauty, there are simply no adjectives and vocabulary in my dictionary which can be used to describe hyphenate actress, Zoe Tay. Who could forget the inaugural *Star Search Contest* when Zoe, with her confidence and dexterity, came up triumphant and became one of television's favourite actresses.

I was extremely flattered when Zoe agreed to an interview with me. Despite her influence and achievement, Zoe certainly did not exude a diva personality. On the contrary, she was very polite and sincerely answered the questions throughout our conversation.

1988 was possibly one of the highlights of Zoe's glittering career. It marked the start of our very own local talent scouting show in which Zoe strode confidently on her way to the crown and a 3-year contract with what was then known as the Singapore Broadcasting Corporation (SBC). Already a top super-model at that time, Zoe had wanted to learn about show-business and enhance her profile for her already glowing modeling resume. Ironically, she had intended to venture overseas to further her modelling career following the show, and did not put any expectations on herself for the contest, which she confessed helped to overcome her stage fright.

Zoe confided that she felt depressed and lost because she had to change her modelling plans and was not sure if she was able to meet viewers' expectations since as the contest winner. She felt that she had so much to prove and learn, such as memorizing lines, immersing into a certain role, positioning in front of the camera, lighting and acting crew, and Zoe soon started having cold feet. She once raised the idea of quitting show business to her superior as she felt that the other contestants were doing much better than she was.

Barely starting her acting career, Zoe was already counting down the number of days and hoping that she could finish her contract sooner. It was made worse with the enduring long hours and lack of sleep during filming.

She found solace in senior actors and actresses who advised Zoe to observe and learn from her other colleagues like how they moved, how they behaved and how they sounded when they were acting. She recalled how these seniors had shared with her on preparing for a new role, how she had to do her homework and practice her emotions and reactions.

Zoe shared that she consulted a senior actor on how to express feelings and emotions in front of the filming crew easily. The senior actor, whom she did not mention the name, told her that she should *"fall in love a few times, get broken-hearted and then she would be able to know the pain and hurt. By doing so, she would be able to empathize and relate to those emotions for a given role."*

With encouragements from fellow colleagues, Zoe gradually began to enjoy acting and going to work every day was no longer a chore. She learned from her seniors and prepared for her roles conscientiously. Zoe's love for acting still flames brightly today after 20 years, and she is still learning something new about acting every day.

Pretty Faces, though, was a game-changer for Zoe. The 30-parter drama serial catapulted her into stardom. Casted a very materialistic and vindictive character *Bobo*, it was a character you would love, hate and empathize. In an era where female actresses were predominantly casted into conservative roles, *Bobo* challenged the stereotype as an outspoken, raunchy and sexy female. It was not only until *Pretty Faces* that actresses started to show more "skin" on television. This was, however, not without its sacrifices.

For one, Zoe had to learn smoking. It was a character contradictory to her real life, and something that she was totally unaccustomed to, but Zoe felt that she had to bring out Bobo's loud and mercenary character on-screen or the character would be mundane and lifeless. Zoe observed and researched on the role intensely. She wanted to bring out Bobo's salacious character in a time when skin and lewd scenes were likely scorned at and would never make it on television in Singapore.

It was through Zoe's courage, tenacity and spunk that she brought out the mercenary and amoral side of *Bobo* on the screen. Zoe conceded that many people perceived *Bobo* to be similar to her real life, which speaks volumes of her portrayal in reel life. She shared that in real life, unless she was doing a photo-shoot, Zoe would usually wear conservative t-shirts and jeans with comfortable footwear.

Needless to say, *Pretty Faces* was a great success, stamping her success on the screens. She received many compliments for her role as Bobo and the compliments which Zoe received contributed to her increased self-confidence as an actress. Beyond a shadow of doubt, Zoe is a brilliant and gifted actress.

After 3 years, Zoe finally felt that she had completed a really good acting project. After the success of *Pretty Faces*, she received more television and film projects and was constantly on magazines and media. The press and her fans began to crown and label her as the *Queen of Caldecott Hill*. Whatever label she was given, Zoe was industrious and gave her best shot at every acting project she was given.

In 1995, Zoe was at the peak of her career and she became the first female artiste to launch a coffee table book titled "Zoe's Coffee table". The coffee table book was commissioned by MediaCorp and Zoe herself labelled the coffee table book as "JUICY". She felt that the book failed to reflect the true Zoe. It was another coffee table book with beautiful and sensual pictures of Zoe, but it was not a true reflection of her story. Zoe divulged that on hindsight, if she had another opportunity, she would like to work with Wee Khim, one of Singapore's most prolific and iconic photographers, to come up with another coffee table book. It would be filled with her past and present, living through the years and tears, captured in words and pictures.

Zoe has been well-known and touted as a "chameleon" actress for her versatility, talent and audacity to try out many different roles. I asked Zoe a very simple question on how she connects with and capture the essence of each character. Zoe said she took up some acting classes and she observes people from her everyday life.

Everyone walks and talks differently, adding that no two persons say "Good Morning" in the same manner.

Clearly a media and fan favourite, Zoe has been a constant fixture at the *Star Awards* since 1994, as one of the most accomplished and talented actresses. Zoe was the first actress to have acted in Singapore's only drama trilogy, *The Unbeatables* and also won the Best Actress Award in 1996 for her stellar and outstanding role in *The Golden Pillow*, in which she acted alongside Hong Kong's Alex Man. In 1998, she was awarded the Special Achievement Award for her acting contribution to the local scene. Furthermore, Zoe's outstanding performance in *Home Affairs* and *The Ultimatum* also earned her nominations for Best Drama Performance by an Actress at the Asian TV Awards in 2000 and 2009 respectively.

For Zoe, being a media darling comes with her job as an actress and she was even more exposed to the media since she was casted in so many television and film roles. At the peak of her career in 1995, Zoe registered her marriage with her pilot boyfriend, Philip Chionh so that they can purchase a house. Six years later in 2001, Zoe finally walked down the aisle with her prince in a church wedding coupled with a captivating western –styled dinner at Ritz-Carlton Hotel.

There were always critics who thought that it was at the peak of her career and that it was too soon to get hitched, but Zoe felt she was ready to get married, have a house and start a family. Prior to the church wedding and dinner, Zoe spoke to MediaCorp's CEO that she hoped for her wedding to be a private affair and not televised because her husband was not a celebrity nor was he someone from the entertainment industry.

For Zoe and her husband, privacy is the best policy. While many friends and colleagues were invited to the church wedding, there were only 60 to 80 seats meant for family, friends and colleagues at her wedding dinner party. Zoe wanted the western military wedding because it was refined and unpresumptuous. Furthermore,

Zoe had a western-style wedding with eight long tables and the seating arrangement was, as she puts it, a "headache".

Over the years, Zoe learnt to understand the media and conversely, let the media and fans understand her. She refrained from reading unnecessary negative reports of herself and kept her family matters very private to abstain from causing unnecessary distress to her family and herself.

After Zoe had her Church Wedding and wedding dinner, she wanted a "honeymoon period" of two years to spend time with her partner. Being a military pilot, her husband was not around most of the time and had to go on frequent work trips. Given work commitments, she put off having children until she was 35 years old. It took her two years to get pregnant with her first baby and she had to try even harder for their second child, which came four years later. Having had two boys, Zoe and her husband went on to try for a baby girl at the age of 42, and I really admire her for her fearlessness to try for another baby after 40 because of the known pregnancy complications for older women. She chuckled that all she did was adding another baby brother to her children.

Zoe encourages women to get married early before 30 if they plan to have kids. By 30, they should start having children and by 40, "it's time for the women to get pretty again," said Zoe. It is because when you are older, it is more difficult for you to conceive and there are more dangers for pregnant women above 35 years old. At a more mature age, you will also have less stamina and energy level to catch up with your kids. Zoe recounted that besides the financial stability, you must also be mentally prepared to have kids. You must also be committed to be a parent as parenthood is certainly not easy. Zoe reiterated that, "I am very blessed to have 3 boys; they are healthy, naughty but naturally they are boys. The Singapore Government is also encouraging working mothers to have more children. After I have become a mother, I have become more realistic and I need to do a lot of planning for my family."

Zoe hopes to inculcate more Chinese values in her children. She wants her children to have more manners and also bonding as a family. Zoe puts a lot of attention on her children's behaviour. If her boys come back and are behaving badly, Zoe will always communicate with their teacher. After a hard day's work, all Zoe wants is to return home to her kids and play with them. Zoe also tries to get her kids to be more interested in Chinese. She even recommended me this show called _Xi Yang Yang_ which I shared with my second son, Charles, and he was instantly and immediately enticed by the aforesaid Chinese Children's Educational Series.

For working women struggling with family and their career, Zoe feels that spousal and familial support is very important. It will be an uphill struggle if the woman does not have any spousal or family encouragement and support.

Zoe feels that as women, we are able to take up a leading role in our career but because we have to sacrifice so much of our time to take care for our family that we sometimes neglect our career and it takes a backseat. She deems that we have a maternal instinct and calling after we have our children and thus as women, we spend a lot of time nurturing and parenting our children. As for the men, Zoe still considers them to be the lead financial provider for the family.

Nonetheless, Zoe has been extremely modest with her achievements. She has been an A-list actress with MediaCorp for more than two decades and it takes a lot hard work to get to where she is today. Zoe has broken many boundaries over the two decades as an actress with MediaCorp and she has shown many that she is a talented and gifted actress. She has an industrious and independent personality, and has been able to conscientiously manage her time, career and family life in an outstanding manner.

Zoe Tay — actress, icon, legend, Extraordinary Woman.

CONCLUSION

The book project started in 2012 because I felt that Singaporean women have been treated inadequately by their employers, colleagues and even their lifelong partners. Therefore, I started on this book project to interview well-known Singaporean female entrepreneurs, professionals and media personalities so that the readers of my book can connect to these female interviewees more easily.

I hope that the book can motivate, inspire and encourage women in our society to dream big, to step out and step up. However, to achieve their final dreams and goals, men will have to play a part in supporting women in their workplace or at home. Many talented women have decided to stay put at one position and not climb the career ladder simply because they lack the encouragement at their workplace and at home. It is frustrating to see women holding back because of narrow-minded stereotyping.

True gender equality exists only when women rise to the top of most government sectors or corporations and women should work hard to get there. However, this can only happen when both men and women accept and recognize that stereotyping and biases only impair our judgment. Rather than ignoring our differences, both genders should embrace our differences.

In our present situation, even though we have come a long way to be a first-world nation, gender inequality still exists unless women receive more support from their employers, the Government, family and their lifelong partners in terms of equal salaries, equal working conditions, child-bearing and child-rearing. Today, men should contribute equally to maintaining the household and also child-rearing.

Women should also work together and look out for each other and by doing so, can we then achieve more voice and more success in attaining gender equality. Sometimes, it is discouraging to see women compete against one another instead of collaborating. They question each other's leadership qualities and their commitment towards their jobs. Women should help one another and form a strong alliance to pursue gender equality and achieve fruitful results.

Although women have fought many wars against their better half, it is deplorable that women pick up fights against each other. The worst fight is the one between working mothers and stay-at-home mothers. When Yahoo's CEO, Marissa Mayer was employed by Yahoo in her third trimester, many were surprised. However, this opened the door for pregnant women to be employed by major corporations. As work was tough being a new CEO, Mayer only took a couple of weeks of maternity leave after the birth of her first child.

Mayer came under fire from mother groups as she took only couple of weeks of maternity leave when most Silicon Valley female employees take 4 to 5 months of maternity leave. Many asked, "What was she trying to prove?" Shortly after the fiasco, Marissa banned all employees from working from home. Marissa said, "She said that Yahoo needed people in the office in order to be more collaborative."

While most Yahoo employees seemed to support the decision, many business critics outside the company and several employees inside of Yahoo abhorred Mayer's ban which made life harder for Yahoo's working mothers. Several female employees were also upset that Mayer had built an in-house nursery in her office which was too extravagant and seemingly she is the only one doing it in office.

However, I understood Mayer's decision to take a short few weeks of maternity leave from work. She was the President and CEO of one of the largest technology firms in the world and she had to make many decisions to make and answer for as the President and CEO. Mayer could not possibly take a 5-month maternity leave because she has the Board of Directors to account for and shouldering too much responsibility to take a long maternity leave. Besides being the President and CEO of Yahoo, Mayer is also a new mother and building a nursery in her office at her own expense, provided her some time to spend with her little boy.

In order to achieve gender equality, government bodies and corporations should start to employ more female in leadership positions. They should commit to support changing the leadership roles ratio. Companies can also promote within. Government bodies and companies can sponsor female employees to take up more courses and even pay for their college or masters degrees.

It is time for us to march forward and realize gender equality. Gender equality is long overdue and it should be our fight to make sure true gender equality is evident in Government bodies, Multi-National Companies, Academia, Law Firms, Hospitals, Arts and Culture. Besides encouraging gender equality at work, society should also change their views about stay-at-home fathers. The motivation is to strive towards a society where gender inequality is no longer the social norm. We will see fathers dropping off their children at school or extra-curricular activities and mothers busy at work. We should be differentiated not by our gender but by our passion, talents and interests. Only when humanity works together can gender equality be achieved.

Printed in the United States
By Bookmasters